VOICES OF THE TITANIC

HISTORY SPEAKS!

VOICES OF THE TITANIC

A *TITANIC* BOOK FOR KIDS

MARY MONTERO

ROCKRIDGE
PRESS

To all the men, women, and children aboard the *Titanic* and the historians who have painstakingly kept her memory alive.

Interior and Cover Designer: Stephanie Sumulong

Art Producer: Janice Ackerman

Editor. Laura Bryn Sisson

Production Editor: Mia Moran

Production Manager: Giraud Lorber

Cover Photography: top middle: Bettmann/Getty Images; top right: George Grantham Bain Collection, Library of Congress; middle: George Grantham Bain Collection, Library of Congress; bottom: Universal History Archive/UIG/Bridgeman Images.

Interior Photography: p.16: New York World-Telegram and the Sun Newspaper Photograph Collection, Library of Congress; p. 21: Artindo/Shutterstock; p. 22: Harris & Ewing Collection, Library of Congress; p. 23: Library of Congress; p.26: Private Collection/Bridgeman Images; p. 30: Time Life Pictures/Getty Images; p. 32: © Ken Welsh / Bridgeman Images; p.35: Bettmann/Getty Images; p.37: The Titanic Collection/UIG/Bridgeman Images; p. 38: Private Collection/Prismatic Pictures/Bridgeman Images; p. 45: Harris & Ewing Collection, Library of Congress; p. 47: The Titanic Collection/UIG/ Bridgeman Images; p.49: Private Collection/Prismatic Pictures/Bridgeman Images; p. 51: © Phil Yeomans/BNPS; p. 56: National Geographic Image Collection/Bridgeman Images; p. 57: The Titanic Collection/UIG/ Bridgeman Images; p. 58: © George Rinhart/Corbis Historical/Getty Images; p. 70: George Grantham Bain Collection, Library of Congress; p. 72: National Archives; p. 84: © David Paul Morris/Getty Images; p. 86: George Grantham Bain Collection, Library of Congress; p. 87: National Archives; p. 91: The Titanic Collection/UIG/Bridgeman Images; p. 96: Bettmann/Getty Images; p. 99: George Grantham Bain Collection, Library of Congress; p. 100: Bettmann/Getty Images; p. 105: George Grantham Bain Collection, Library of Congress; p. 108: Library of Congress

ISBN: Print 978-1-64152-978-5 | eBook 978-1-64152-979-2

R0

CONTENTS

INTRODUCTION

Can you pinpoint what about the *Titanic* captured your interest and led you to pick up this book? Is it the vastness of the unthinkable tragedy? Do you yearn to know more about the people on board? Is it the discovery of the wreckage two miles beneath the ocean?

Since the night of the fateful sinking, the *Titanic*'s story has enchanted both the young and the old. The *Titanic* changed the face of history, and her story yearns to be told and retold.

Exactly what happened on the ship remains a puzzle. The *Titanic* sailed and sank in an era without social media and smartphones. Other than the decaying wreckage lying 12,500 feet underwater, the only evidence is found in the firsthand stories of the survivors, all of whom have now passed away. Every passenger on board the *Titanic* had a unique perspective on what happened that night. Stories of heroism, circumstance, bravery, and cowardice all rose with the sun the morning after the sinking.

These stories come from the memories of traumatized survivors. It's important to keep in mind that survivor accounts were sometimes contradictory, as many firsthand accounts of disturbing events can be. Chaos marred the evening, and memories were often fuzzy or became embellished as years passed.

This book tells the stories of the passengers and crew members who boarded the ship of dreams, some of whom would never leave it. The 20 biographies you read here give a small glimpse into the terror that unfolded for crew members and passengers that night. Get ready to learn about the harrowing moments Frederick Fleet experienced in the **crow's nest** and the tireless efforts of Harold Bride and Jack Phillips in the wireless room. Prepare to put yourself in the shoes of first-class passengers like Margaret Brown. Expect to imagine life aboard the ship like third-class passenger Frankie Goldsmith, who was just nine years old when the ship went down.

Use the glossary to help navigate some of the trickier ship-related terms in the book, which will be in **bold** the first time you see them.

As you read, remember that these individual stories will help you put together one monumental tale. We can learn a lot about history through the eyes of the people who were there.

RMS *TITANIC:*
THE UNSINKABLE SHIP

Great fanfare marked the RMS *Titanic*'s maiden voyage. Never before had a passenger **liner** drawn so much attention for its size and luxury. It was the largest ship that had ever sailed the ocean, weighing over 46,000 tons, with a length of 882 feet, 9 inches.

BUILDING THE SISTER SHIPS

In 1907, the White Star Line dreamed up three record-breaking ocean liners. The ships would serve as Royal Mail Steamers, transporting mail to and from America. They would also carry passengers in unprecedented luxury.

To design the ships, White Star commissioned shipbuilders Harland and Wolff. On July 29, 1908, the chairman of the White Star Line, J. Bruce Ismay, was presented with plans for the ships and gave his stamp of approval. Construction on the RMS *Olympic* started in December 1908. The RMS *Titanic* followed on March 31, 1909. It took 15,000 shipbuilders 26 months to complete the ships.

On June 14, 1911, the *Olympic* set sail on her maiden voyage under the direction of Captain Edward John Smith. On her fifth voyage and still under the command of Captain Smith, the *Olympic* collided with a Navy

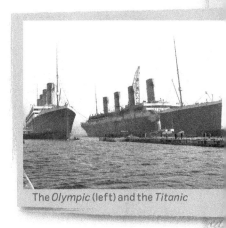

The *Olympic* (left) and the *Titanic*

ship, causing her severe damage. Not only did this take the *Olympic* out of service, but the repairs took away space and workers from the construction of the *Titanic*, delaying her launch from March 20 to April 10, 1912.

Making White Star's dreams become reality wasn't cheap. Building the *Titanic* cost $7.5 million (over $166 million today). The ship also came at a human cost. During the *Titanic*'s construction, over 246 injuries occurred, and nine men died.

On March 31, 1911, the *Titanic* was brought to a fitting-out berth to decorate the interior. With all of her finishing touches in place, the *Titanic* departed Southampton, England, for her intended destination of New York. The ship made stops in Cherbourg, France, and Queenstown, Ireland, where more passengers boarded the ship and a lucky few disembarked.

What about the final ship of the trio? Construction on the *Britannic* began in November 1911. She was still under construction when the *Titanic* disaster occurred. The resulting changes made to ships delayed the *Britannic*'s construction. By the time she launched, World War I had begun, and she ran as a hospital ship. In 1916, the *Britannic* struck a mine and sank in 55 minutes, making her the largest ship lost in the war.

UNSINKABLE

While the White Star Line never claimed that the *Titanic* was unsinkable, the public hailed her as the most reliable ship ever at sea. This claim came in part due to the *Titanic* and the *Olympic*'s state-of-the-art design, which included 16 compartments in the **hull** with doors that could be closed to keep water in one section from flowing into other sections. Containing inrushing water and preventing it from flooding the rest of the ship would help keep the ship from sinking. But these compartments weren't truly watertight. The doors reached up to above the ship's waterline, but they did not reach the top of the compartments. If one compartment overflowed, water would spill over into the next one.

THE CLASSES

With three distinct classes, the *Titanic* had a place on board for everyone. First-class passengers could spend their days in the swimming pool or the gym, or relaxing in the library. Second-class passengers played shuffleboard, drank tea, and wrote letters, while third-class passengers enjoyed games on the **deck**, music, and dance parties.

Passage wasn't cheap no matter which class you occupied. In today's prices, a first-class cabin cost $3,500; the most expensive parlor suites cost $100,000. A cabin in second class would cost about $1,375 today, whereas one in third class would cost between $350 and $900.

The *Titanic's* first-class lounge

First-class cabins were located in the middle of the ship, protected from rocking and ship noise, and had heated rooms and private bathrooms. While second class wasn't as extravagant, passengers still experienced amenities not offered by many other ships, such as a library, a dining saloon, and three outdoor decks. Many middle-class families took passage in second class.

Though third-class accommodations, also known as **steerage**, might not seem luxurious by today's standards, they were some of the finest in their class at that time. Third-class passengers were often immigrants moving to America in search of a better life. Their cabins were located on the lower decks and were subject to more engine noise, the rocking of the ship, and vibrations. There were only two bathtubs in steerage to accommodate its more than 700 passengers!

THE SINKING

The evening of April 14 was calm and clear. When the *Titanic*'s hull rumbled across the iceberg at 11:40 p.m., many passengers were asleep, and others relaxed on the decks or socialized in the first-class lounge. Most passengers in first class felt only a jolt. Some noticed the engines come to a stop, but many didn't think anything of it. Passengers on the deck played with chunks of ice that fell on board. Nobody thought they were in any imminent danger.

Passengers and crew in the lower decks, closer to the gashes that the iceberg tore into the hull, felt the true impact. Engine oiler Walter Hurst remembered being awoken "by a grinding crash along the **starboard** side. No one was very much alarmed but knew we had struck something."

Captain Edward John Smith could tell something was very wrong. The sound of the accident woke him, and he headed to the **bridge**. He and shipbuilder Thomas Andrews assessed the situation, noting that the ship was already tilting down at the head just moments after it had struck the iceberg.

As the men investigated, they found the mail room, cargo holds, and squash court already flooded, along with several boiler rooms. Water was pouring into the ship 15 times faster than it could be pumped out. Icy water blasted crew members in the boiler room, where the iceberg had torn the hull—they barely escaped before the crew on the bridge closed the watertight doors remotely.

It quickly became clear that the *Titanic* had sustained serious damage. She was designed to stay afloat with four of the watertight compartments flooded. The impact with the iceberg punctured the **forward** six compartments, dooming the ship.

Smith and Andrews knew that a sinking ship was only the first half of the tragedy. Due to lenient regulations and a desire for open space on the decks, the liner carried only 20 **lifeboats**, capable of evacuating 1,178 people. There were over 2,200 on board.

Once they realized how dire the situation was, crew members scrambled to fill the lifeboats with women and children, but many of the boats left the ship half-empty. Scores of passengers thought they'd be safer on the grand ship than on a small lifeboat out at sea.

The Titanic sank rapidly, with only 2 hours and 40 minutes between the collision and the sinking at 2:20 a.m. on April 15, 1912. When the Titanic sank, hundreds of people plunged into the icy waters of the Atlantic. Some were trapped below the decks of the ship. Most passengers in the open water were wearing **lifebelts**, so they didn't immediately drown. Instead, they froze to death due to the frigid water temperatures. Survivors on the lifeboats, many of whom had lost their spouses or children, watched the scene in horror as they waited for hours for help to arrive.

Having received the *Titanic*'s calls for help, the rescue ship *Carpathia* was steaming toward the *Titanic* as fast as she could. She arrived by 4:00 a.m. to begin rescuing survivors.

Over the next several days, the *Titanic*'s survivors scoured the decks of the *Carpathia*, hoping to reunite with lost loved ones. For most, those reunions never came. More than 1,500 people died in the middle of the Atlantic that night.

THE AFTERMATH

The tragedy forever changed the face of sea travel. British and American investigations sought to piece together enough information to determine exactly what happened and recommend changes to prevent future catastrophes. Surviving crew members and several passengers were questioned at length about the events leading up to, during, and following the disaster.

After the inquiries, governments quickly enacted new maritime laws. All passenger ships were required to carry enough lifeboats for all passengers and crew,

The World.

GREAT TITANIC SINKS; MORE THAN 1,500 LOST;
866 WOMEN AND CHILDREN KNOWN TO BE SAVED;
SCORES OF NOTABLES NOT ACCOUNTED FOR

LIST OF THE KNOWN SAVED

Front page of *The World* newspaper, April 16, 1912

have a human-operated radio 24 hours a day, and carry searchlights on board.

In the years that followed, many survivors gave informal interviews, helping the story live on. When Robert Ballard found the sunken ship two miles beneath the ocean in 1985, public interest surged. James Cameron's blockbuster film *Titanic*, released in 1997, also caused an explosion of renewed curiosity.

People clamored for information. Survivors of the shipwreck, by that time in their eighties and nineties, became instant celebrities.

Many historians have made it their mission to never let the stories of the *Titanic* get lost in time. You are now a crucial part of making sure they live on. As you immerse yourself in the stories that follow, always hold the memory of the *Titanic* in your heart and remember the many thousands who were forever affected by her loss.

THE SHIP

LENGTH: 882 feet, 9 inches
WEIGHT: 46,328 tons
TOP SPEED: 24 knots
ROOMS: 840
LIFEBOAT CAPACITY: 1,178 people
LIFEBELTS: 3,560

THE PEOPLE

MAXIMUM CAPACITY: 3,547 passengers and crew
APPROXIMATE NUMBER OF PEOPLE ON BOARD: 2,200
PASSENGERS: 1,317
    FIRST CLASS: 324
    SECOND CLASS: 285
    THIRD CLASS: 708

**APPROXIMATE NUMBER OF
PEOPLE WHO PERISHED:** more than 1,500

NOTE: US inquiry determined 1,517 lives were lost.
British inquiry determined 1,503 lives were lost.

THE *TITANIC'S* HIGH-RANKING CREW MEMBERS

(Those in italics survived.)

CAPTAIN/COMMANDER: Edward John Smith, 62

CHIEF OFFICER: Lieutenant Henry Tingle Wilde, 39

FIRST OFFICER: Lieutenant William McMaster Murdoch, 39

SECOND OFFICER: Sublieutenant Charles Herbert Lightoller, 38

THIRD OFFICER: Herbert John Pitman, 34

FOURTH OFFICER: Sublieutenant Joseph Groves Boxhall, 28

FIFTH OFFICER: Sublieutenant Harold Godfrey Lowe, 29

SIXTH OFFICER: Sublieutenant James Paul Moody, 24

SHIPBUILDER: Thomas Andrews, 39

CHAIRMAN OF THE WHITE STAR LINE: Bruce Ismay, 49

OTHER NOTABLE NAMES

CAPTAIN ROSTRON: Captain of the *Carpathia*, the *Titanic*'s rescue ship

ROBERT BALLARD: Discovered the wreck of the *Titanic* in 1985

THE JOURNEY

September 1, 1985: Wreck of the *Titanic* found.

April 14, 1912, 11:40 p.m.: The *Titanic* collides with the iceberg.

HALIFAX

NEW YORK

April 15, 1912, 4:10 a.m.: The rescue ship *Carpathia* reaches the first lifeboat.

April 15, 1912, 2:20 a.m.: The *Titanic* sinks.

April 15, 1912, 12:15 a.m.: The *Carpathia* receives the *Titanic's* distress call

April 19 to May 25, 1912: American inquiry into the disaster.

May 2 to July 3, 1912: British inquiry into the disaster.

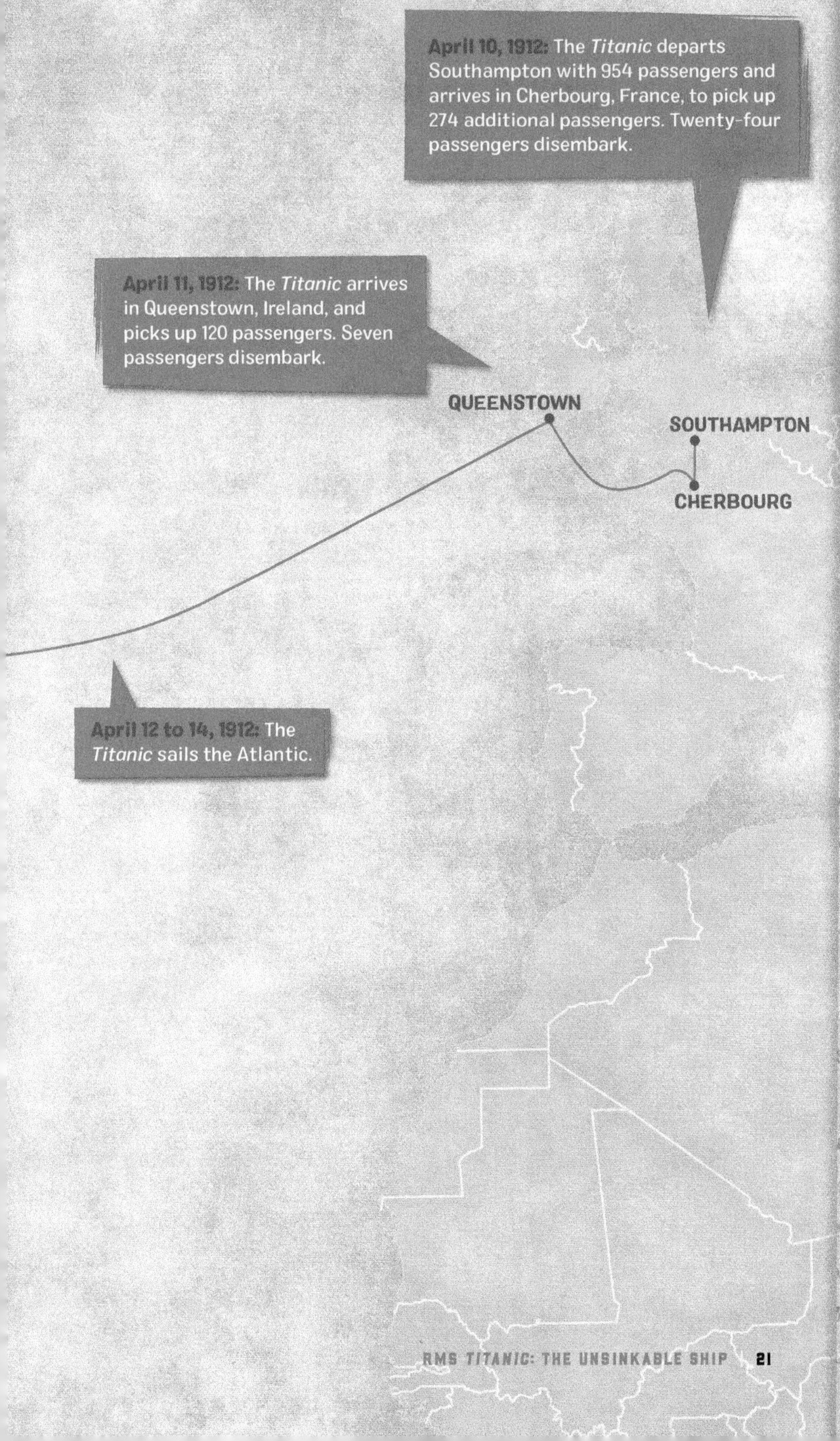

April 10, 1912: The *Titanic* departs Southampton with 954 passengers and arrives in Cherbourg, France, to pick up 274 additional passengers. Twenty-four passengers disembark.

April 11, 1912: The *Titanic* arrives in Queenstown, Ireland, and picks up 120 passengers. Seven passengers disembark.

QUEENSTOWN

SOUTHAMPTON

CHERBOURG

April 12 to 14, 1912: The *Titanic* sails the Atlantic.

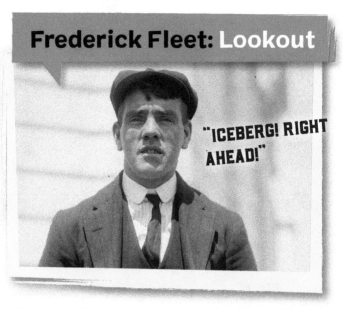

Frederick Fleet: Lookout

"ICEBERG! RIGHT AHEAD!"

Before boarding the *Titanic* as a lookout, Fleet, a longtime seaman, had served on the *Titanic*'s **sister ship**, the *Oceanic*. His job was to keep a sharp eye on the waters through which the ship traveled.

On the night of April 14, 1912, Fleet and his partner, Reginald Robinson Lee, climbed the ladder nearly 15 meters above the **forecastle deck** to the **crow's nest**. From there they had a clear view of the ocean. They were reporting for their 10:00 p.m. to midnight shift on a bitterly cold night. The pair, known as a watch group, took heed of the ice warnings from the group that had previously been on duty that night. Colleagues Archie Jewell and George Symons warned them of looming danger, recommending that they keep "a sharp lookout for small ice."

Fleet and Lee maintained a watchful eye on the ocean, with only the starry, moonless sky to light the waters between the ship and the horizon. The crew relied on their unassisted eyesight to detect any approaching danger. The lookouts on the *Titanic* were not using binoculars. Although the reason has never been confirmed, it is a widely held belief that the binoculars were locked in a supply cabinet. The key to that cabinet had been accidentally taken off the ship the day before the *Titanic*'s departure.

At 11:40 p.m., the men squinted as the black outline of the infamous iceberg came into view. As soon as he realized what he was looking at, Fleet rang the crow's nest bell three times. He called the bridge, warning

The iceberg that sank the *Titanic*, as photographed from the *Carpathia*

them, "Iceberg! Right ahead!" The commander on the bridge thanked him.

From their perch high above the deck, all the men could do was wait and watch. Shortly after Fleet's call to the bridge, the lookouts felt the iceberg graze the side of the ship and watched as chunks of ice fell along the deck. At that point, the lookouts believed the iceberg had merely scraped against the side of the boat.

Fleet and Lee continued to occupy their spot in the crow's nest until midnight, then headed down to the decks to help load lifeboats. Fleet was quickly instructed to board lifeboat 6 to help captain the boat, ensuring his safe return to New York.

Following the disaster, during the US inquiry, authorities quizzed Fleet about the missing binoculars. Fleet admitted that with them, they would have been able to see the iceberg sooner. When asked how much sooner, he responded, "Well, enough to get out of the way."

WHO'S WHO

David Blair, the seaman who had the key to the locker where the binoculars were kept, had planned to be on board the ship during the maiden voyage. The White Star Line removed him from his position on the *Titanic* at the last minute, and he accidentally took the key with him.

WHO KNEW

The three pairs of lookouts aboard the *Titanic* worked in two-hour shifts around the clock. Fleet and Lee were on duty from 4:00 a.m. to 6:00 a.m. and 10:00 a.m. to noon, then 4:00 p.m. to 6:00 p.m. and 10:00 p.m. to midnight. All the lookouts survived the sinking.

Jack Phillips and Harold Bride: Wireless Operators

"COME AT ONCE. WE HAVE STRUCK A BERG."

The wireless room aboard a similar liner to the *Titanic*

C ommunicating with the rest of the world while steaming across the Atlantic Ocean was no easy task. The only way was via the Marconi system, a relatively new transatlantic radio telegraph technology created by Guglielmo Marconi. This wireless technology allowed the transmission of messages from ship to shore and was the ship's only link to the outside world.

Jack Phillips, senior wireless operator, and Harold Bride, junior operator, were at the controls of this high-tech communication device on board the *Titanic*.

Their primary job was to send and receive messages for passengers who paid for the service.

Although the operators reported to Captain Smith, they were employees of the Marconi Wireless Company, not the White Star Line. Sending and receiving messages regarding the ship's business was second priority behind paid passenger messages. Bride believed they transmitted over 250 messages during the journey, and on April 14, 1912, the wireless system stopped working due to overuse. Advised to wait for a repair when they arrived in New York, Bride and Phillips instead spent hours working to fix the problem. They eventually got the system up and running and spent many more hours catching up on the messages that had piled up.

In their rush, the men overlooked two messages that would have relayed pivotal information to the captain. Bride and Phillips later faced sharp criticism for their lack of response to these ice warnings, which may have changed the *Titanic*'s course—and history.

The first missed message was sent to the *Titanic* from a nearby ship, the *Mesaba*, only three hours before the *Titanic* struck the iceberg. The note told of "heavy pack ice and [a] great number of large icebergs" in the vicinity. According to speculation, the radio operators missed the message because the sending ship forgot to add the prefix "MSG." This telegraph code meant "Masters' Service Gram" and would have required receipt by Captain Smith.

Forty minutes before the collision, the *Californian* sent a message to the *Titanic*. The *Californian* was stuck in a dangerous ice field in the middle of the *Titanic*'s course. This message warned that the *Californian* was stopped because the conditions were too treacherous. An exhausted Jack Phillips intercepted this message and replied with Morse code, "D-D-D," which reads as "shut up." Captain Smith never received either of these warnings.

Despite overlooking these messages, the work Phillips and Bride did after the collision was crucial to the fate of the survivors. During the hours after the ship hit the iceberg, the men tirelessly contacted nearby ships to let them know of their peril and begged for assistance. "**CQD**" and "SOS" were both recognizable distress signals, and the men desperately tapped them out, along with "MGY," the *Titanic*'s call signal.

"Come at once. We have struck a berg. It's a CQD, old man."

"Come as quickly as possible, old man: The engine room is filling up to the boilers."

"This is *Titanic*. CQD. Engine room flooded."

"We are in collision with berg. Sinking head down. Come soon as possible."

The closest ship was the *Californian*, the same ship they had gruffly told off less than an hour before. Her wireless crew had since turned off the radios for the night, and the operator had gone to bed. The next nearest ship, the *Carpathia*, was some 58 miles from the *Titanic*. Her wireless operator, who was just about to turn in for the night, noticed the messages and raced the distress calls to the captain, who quickly changed course. The *Carpathia* steamed toward the *Titanic*'s last given location, with its wireless operators giving periodic updates on their progress.

Phillips and Bride tapped out message after message, hoping to find someone to rescue passengers before the ship sank. After the crew had lowered the final lifeboat, Captain Smith reportedly went to the wireless room and told the operators, "Men, you have done all you can. You can do no more. Abandon your cabin. Now it's every man for himself." For 15 more minutes, Phillips continued to tap out distress codes along with their location.

The last distress message sent from the *Titanic* read, "CQD CQD SOS SOS CQD DE MGY MGY."

Bride and Phillips left their post just moments before the ship went down. Bride plunged into the icy water and was momentarily trapped under collapsible lifeboat B, which had overturned. He eventually managed to balance on top of it.

Rescuers helping Harold Bride off the *Carpathia*

Phillips, who treaded water in an attempt to survive, ended up clinging to the same collapsible lifeboat. But after being exposed to the frigid waters for so long, Phillips's body quietly slipped into the ocean sometime before dawn.

As the night wore on, after most victims had already succumbed to hypothermia, other nearby wireless operators received word of the disaster. They sent hopeful messages to the ship, which had already sunk. One ship sent a message to the *Titanic* around 3:00 a.m., nearly an hour after she had dropped to the ocean floor. The message read, "Steaming full speed for you ... hope you are safe." This haunting message never arrived.

WHO'S WHO

After the sinking, Marconi was celebrated as a hero. His technology had helped save lives. Marconi also narrowly avoided death: The White Star Line had offered him free passage on the *Titanic*'s maiden voyage, but he had declined.

WHO KNEW

Collapsible lifeboat B overturned before its launch. All who clung to it—many of them male crew members—were exposed to freezing water. Lifeboats 4 and 12 rescued the men after hearing **Officer** Lightoller whistle for help. Had those lifeboats not come to the rescue, the occupants of boat B would have all frozen to death.

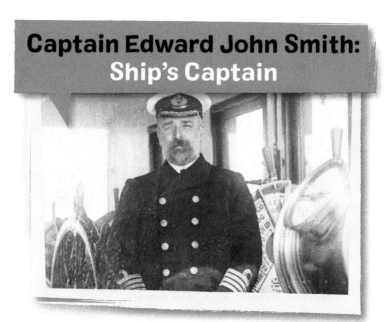

Captain Edward John Smith:
Ship's Captain

In 1880, Edward John Smith joined the White Star Line, one of the most prominent shipping companies in the world. Smith spent the rest of his career working for the company, commanding 18 ships before taking over the helm of the *Titanic*. Over his 43 years at sea, Smith rose in seniority and gained the trust of passengers and shipmates. He was so well-known, many refused to sail the Atlantic without him in command. He was dubbed "the millionaire's captain," as wealthy passengers had a particular fondness for him.

On the morning of April 10, 1912, Captain Smith boarded the *Titanic* around 7:00 a.m. to prepare for her departure. In the first few moments of the voyage, Smith narrowly avoided a collision with a smaller liner, the *New York*, at the Southampton docks. The swell caused by the *Titanic* caused the ropes holding the *New York* to break free. Careful maneuvering by Smith prevented the ships from colliding. Some passengers saw the near miss as a bad omen for the maiden voyage.

During the remainder of the trip, Captain Smith was well aware of the danger brewing in the Atlantic. He received multiple reports of ice in the area where the ship was sailing. He heeded the first two warnings he received on April 14, ordering a slightly different course for the ship. However, Smith never reduced the ship's speed, cruising along at 22 knots (the equivalent of 25 miles per hour). The ship's maximum speed was 24 knots.

> **"I CANNOT IMAGINE ANY CONDITION WHICH WOULD CAUSE A SHIP TO FOUNDER. MODERN SHIPBUILDING HAS GONE BEYOND THAT."**
> (Captain Smith in 1907)

On the night of the sinking, Smith enjoyed a dinner party in his honor, hosted by first-class passenger

George Widener and attended by some of the wealthiest passengers aboard. Smith left the party at 9:00 p.m. to discuss the ice warnings with Second Officer Charles Lightoller on the bridge. He then retired to his cabin by 9:20 p.m.

Captain Smith was startled awake by a jolt at 11:40 p.m. He raced to the bridge to see what had happened.

When informed of the collision with the iceberg, Smith called for Thomas Andrews, the ship's designer. After examining the damage, Andrews told Smith that the *Titanic* would surely sink.

At 12:05 a.m., after learning that the ship had no chance of survival, Smith ordered the lifeboats to be lowered. He instructed the wireless operators to send out distress calls, and flares were shot high into the sky. Officer Lightoller asked the captain whether women and children should be loaded first, and the commander responded with a solemn nod.

There is much uncertainty regarding the moments that followed the collision. Many people the captain encountered during his final hours perished when the ship sank. This lack of firsthand evidence makes

Captain Smith's actions during his final hours difficult to trace.

Most firsthand accounts paint Captain Smith as being in a state of shock during the 2 hours and 40 minutes that followed the collision with the iceberg. Most agree he was last seen on the bridge just moments before the *Titanic* disappeared into the Atlantic. A now disproven tale told of Smith swimming toward a

Captain Smith looks down from the bridge on lifeboat 1 in this photo taken before the *Titanic* left Queenstown, Ireland

lifeboat with a baby in his hands. **Steward** Edward Brown reported that he and others passed by Smith as the ship sank. The captain called out, "Well, boys, do your best for the women and children, and look out for yourselves."

Captain Smith's body was never found.

WHO'S WHO

Ship designer Thomas Andrews was aboard the *Titanic* to oversee the first voyage and take note of any necessary improvements, which he would apply to the third sister ship, the *Britannic*. On the afternoon of the sinking, Andrews told a friend that the *Titanic* was "nearly as perfect as human brains can make her."

WHO KNEW

Many sources claim Captain Smith considered retirement prior to commanding the *Titanic*. However, a newspaper article published just before the ship's departure stated that Smith would sail the *Titanic* until the White Star Line completed construction on the *Britannic*.

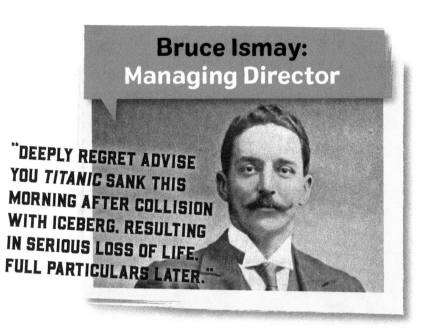

Bruce Ismay: Managing Director

"DEEPLY REGRET ADVISE YOU *TITANIC* SANK THIS MORNING AFTER COLLISION WITH ICEBERG. RESULTING IN SERIOUS LOSS OF LIFE. FULL PARTICULARS LATER."

A businessman at heart, Bruce Ismay was always on the hunt for new opportunities. This drive led him to partner with Harland and Wolff to design and build a trio of ships unlike any others on the ocean. The ships would be faster, their enormous size would trump all others, and their luxury would stun even the richest people. One of those record-shattering ships was the *Titanic*.

Ismay played an important role in the design and building of the *Titanic*. He approved the removal of many of the lifeboats from the ship's design. The original plans Thomas Andrews created allowed for 64 lifeboats—more than enough for everyone on board. Claiming the lifeboats were unsightly, the White Star Line, under Ismay's direction, opted for more open space on the decks—and fewer lifeboats.

Ismay didn't accompany each of his ships on their maiden voyages, but the *Titanic*'s was so momentous that he insisted on going. This fateful choice and the decisions that followed would haunt him for the rest of his life.

The *Titanic's* deck

Throughout the ship's brief journey, passengers overheard Ismay pressuring Captain Smith into cruising at speeds faster than he was comfortable with. Perhaps Ismay was hopeful that the *Titanic* would break speed records and earn even more acclaim.

However, it wasn't only the *Titanic* that would earn notoriety on the night she struck the iceberg. Ismay's actions that night would cement his role as a coward.

The cries of "women and children only!" echoed in the dark as Ismay quietly slipped into collapsible lifeboat C. At 1:40 a.m., the lifeboat was one of the last to depart the sinking ship. As the ship went down, Ismay turned away, unable to face the horror.

Ismay was the highest-ranking White Star Line employee to survive and one of 212 employees to make it out alive. A total of 696 White Star employees went down with the ship.

When they reached the rescue ship *Carpathia*, Ismay demanded a private room, leaving it only once to send a telegram to the White Star Line informing them of the sinking. Other survivors shared cabins with the *Carpathia*'s passengers, slept on the decks, or bunked up in public rooms.

Ismay's reported insistence that Captain Smith make the ship go faster, his presence in a lifeboat that was not completely full, and the way he hid from the misery and mourning aboard the *Carpathia* branded him "the Coward of *Titanic*" and "J. *Brute* Ismay."

No matter how the newspapers attempted to tarnish his name, the official British inquiry into the sinking cleared Ismay of any wrongdoing. It even added that he'd helped save many lives. Although some eyewitnesses claimed there were plenty of women and children nearby who could have taken his spot, Ismay defended his actions—he said there was no one else nearby to board the lifeboat. The boat reached the *Carpathia* carrying 44 passengers, though it could have held 47. The investigation concluded that "had he not jumped in, he would merely have added one more life, namely, his own, to the number of those lost."

There is no proof that Ismay convinced Captain Smith to cruise faster. However, this never completely erased the damage done by the newspaper coverage that followed the disaster. Bruce Ismay lived the remainder of his life out of the spotlight, retiring from the company a year after the sinking. To date, nearly every film and media portrayal of the *Titanic* depicts Ismay as a coward.

WHO KNEW

There were four massive steam funnels on the *Titanic*, one of which was not functional; it was added only to make the ship look even grander. At that time, four funnels represented speed, power, safety, and prestige, so the White Star Line was sure to include all four.

Violet Constance Jessop:
First-Class Stewardess

Violet Jessop while working as a nurse during World War I

urviving the sinking of the *Titanic* was one thing. Surviving the wreck of the *Olympic*, the *Titanic* disaster, and the sinking of the *Britannic* was quite another! Violet Jessop did all three.

Jessop penned several memoirs that detailed her time on all three ships. She wrote that she never wanted to work for the White Star Line, and she wasn't keen on the idea of boarding the *Titanic*. She didn't like sailing in the North Atlantic because of the weather, and she had heard how demanding wealthy passengers could be on lengthy trips. Nevertheless, Jessop ended up on the *Olympic* and survived its minor collision in 1911. She was later persuaded to join the crew of the *Titanic* as a stewardess.

Jessop tended to first-class passengers. Today, we might refer to her job as a maid or housekeeper. She was always at passengers' beck and call. Jessop spent her days cleaning the cabins and attached bathrooms, making beds, running errands, serving tea, and comforting those with seasickness. Her job was exhausting, but she excelled at it for many years.

A first-class stateroom on the *Titanic*, like where Jessop worked

Since her job put her in such close contact with first-class passengers, Jessop had the privilege of getting an intimate glimpse into their lives. Her memoirs detail the attitudes of some of the most famous passengers on the ship. She reminisced about those who were kind and lamented the demanding, callous passengers.

On the night of the sinking, Jessop had finished her day's work and was cozied up in bed with a book. She had almost fallen asleep when she heard a CRASH! She described a "low, rending, crunching, ripping sound, as *Titanic* shivered a trifle and the sound of her engines gently ceased. Quiet, dead silence for a minute. Then doors opened and voices could be heard in gentle enquiry." Jessop shuffled up to the deck, where she was instructed to assist the many non-English-speaking passengers by showing them how to put on their lifebelts and board the lifeboats.

"A FEW WOMEN NEAR ME STARTED TO CRY LOUDLY . . . THEY COULD NOT UNDERSTAND A WORD OF ENGLISH. SURELY A TERRIBLE PLIGHT TO BE AMONG A CROWD IN SUCH A SITUATION AND NOT BE ABLE TO UNDERSTAND ANYTHING THAT IS BEING SAID."

Eventually, Jessop found a spot in lifeboat 16. As the lifeboat began to descend, Jessop later claimed, someone placed a baby in her lap. She clung to the baby throughout the long night. When she finally boarded the *Carpathia*, an unknown woman, likely the baby's mother, came by and swept the baby out of her arms without a word.

Jessop not only survived the sinking of the *Titanic*, but she later went on to survive the sinking of the *Titanic*'s sister ship the *Britannic*. She was on board the vessel working as a nurse during World War I when the *Britannic* sank. She sustained a serious head injury but continued to work for the White Star Line until she retired in 1950. Since her death and the rise in popularity of *Titanic* history, Jessop has been dubbed "Miss Unsinkable."

WHO KNEW

Jessop's memoir mentions that the ship's cat, Jenny, had a litter of kittens a week before the *Titanic* set sail. She took her kittens off the ship just before it left **port**. **Stoker** Jim Mulholland saw this as a bad omen and quickly left. The cat may have saved his life.

John Edward Hart:
Third-Class Steward

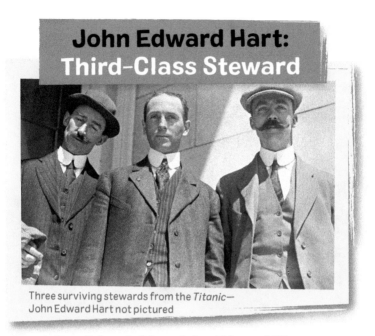

Three surviving stewards from the *Titanic*—
John Edward Hart not pictured

The night of the sinking, John Edward Hart was dozing in his quarters in third class, bunked with 38 other stewards. The jolt of the impact startled the men. The stewards were instructed to wake the passengers for whom they were responsible and warn them. Hart woke up his third-class passengers, helped them put on their lifebelts, and gathered the group in the hallway. They anxiously awaited further instructions.

By 12:30, nearly an hour after the collision, Hart finally received instructions to bring the women and children up to the **boat deck**. As they navigated the maze of hallways, they saw that locking gates separated the third-class passengers from the rest of the ship. Immigration laws required this to prevent the spread of infectious diseases. By the time Hart and his passengers reached the gates, however, they had already been unlocked.

> "THOSE THAT WERE WILLING TO GO TO THE BOAT DECK WERE SHOWN THE WAY.... SOME OF THEM ... THOUGHT THEMSELVES MORE SECURE ON THE SHIP, AND CONSEQUENTLY RETURNED TO THEIR CABIN."

As the *Titanic* filled with water, Hart guided his group up to the boat deck, where they boarded lifeboat 8. It was nearly 1:00 a.m. by the time his group was lowered to safety. The steward then traveled back down to third class and brought another group to lifeboat 15, one of the last boats to leave. As Hart started to head back down to third class to retrieve more passengers, a large group of men—desperate for an escape from the sinking ship—mobbed the lifeboat. Too many people on one lifeboat was dangerous, so Hart helped prevent the men from getting on. First Officer Murdoch, who was loading lifeboats, commanded that Hart board the lifeboat to help row.

Meanwhile, other third-class passengers urgently wound their way through the maze of passageways. Some managed to climb emergency ladders or find back routes to reach the deck and lifeboats, but others got stuck belowdecks, unable to find their way out. Only 172 of 708 third-class passengers survived. Before entering the lifeboat, Hart said, he had single-handedly led 58 of them to safety.

Hart's testimony after the sinking was important in disputing the belief that third-class passengers, who had the lowest survival rate of all passengers, were intentionally left to die. Instead, he confirmed there was simply no policy in place for them. Other areas of the ship received much of the employees' attention during the disaster, while third-class passengers largely had to fend for themselves.

Lifeboat from the *Titanic* arriving at the *Carpathia*

Hart's story became a celebrated tale of heroism after it was recounted in the famous book *A Night to Remember*, authored by Walter Lord in 1955. However, later research revealed inconsistencies in Hart's testimony. For example, only 27 passengers in total occupied lifeboat 8, into which Hart claimed to have placed nearly 30 third-class passengers. Most of its occupants were actually first-class women.

Nobody will ever truly know whether his tale was embellished, fabricated, or marred by the difficulty of remembering such a traumatic event. None of the other third-class stewards survived to corroborate his story.

WHO KNEW

There were 322 male stewards aboard the *Titanic*. Between them, they performed more than 55 jobs throughout the ship, from waiter to housekeeper. Every class had stewards, with one taking care of anywhere from three to 25 rooms.

Wallace Henry Hartley and the Musicians

T he *Titanic*'s performers made up a three-piece trio and a five-piece quintet. A company in charge of placing musicians on British ocean liners assigned the men to work on the ship. They did not work for the White Star Line, and they boarded as second-class passengers, not crew members.

The musicians, whose ages ranged from 20 to 33, were led by violinist Wallace Henry Hartley. They played for first-class passengers at teatime, during after-dinner concerts, and at Sunday church services. On the night of the sinking, the musicians' job changed from providing joy to offering comfort. As soon as passengers began to mill about the decks and common areas, Hartley led the band in a continuous string of songs to lift the hearts of the nervous crowds.

Even as chaos erupted around them, the band played on. They knew the mere presence of music would soothe the passengers' rising anxiety, so they played upbeat songs and old ragtime melodies.

> ## "MUSIC IS A BIGGER WEAPON THAN A GUN IN A BIG EMERGENCY. AND I THINK THAT A BAND COULD DO MORE TO CALM PASSENGERS THAN ALL THE OFFICERS."
> (To a fellow bandmate while serving on another ship)

By the time sheer panic had set in for most passengers, the men moved outside to the boat deck. As the *Titanic* continued her slow tilt into the ocean, they kept playing. Survivors reported that the musicians played even as water began to pour onto the decks.

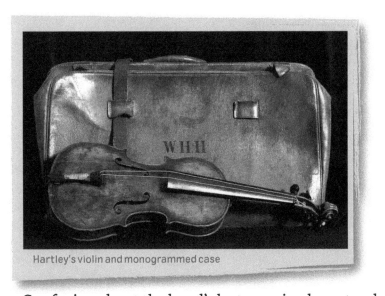
Hartley's violin and monogrammed case

Confusion about the band's last song is a longstanding mystery. Most passengers rescued on lifeboats claim to have heard "Nearer, My God, to Thee." Since most of them left the ship well before the end, it is difficult to know which song was truly the last. The final person who reported hearing the band was Harold Bride, the wireless operator who was on the ship until the very end. He said the band played the song "Autumn" just before they met the icy waters.

In the aftermath of the disaster, survivors praised the band for their fearless work during the terrifying evening. Survivors applauded Hartley for leading the musicians that night, hailing all the men as heroes. No band members survived the sinking.

The *Mackay-Bennett*, a ship tasked with recovering the *Titanic*'s victims, located three of the musicians' bodies. Hartley was found 10 days after the sinking, his music case still strapped to his body. His violin was intact inside the case. It was returned to Hartley's fiancée, Maria Robinson, who had given him the instrument as an engagement present.

In 2006, a relative of the owner rediscovered the violin in an attic in Britain. It was later auctioned off for $1.6 million.

WHO KNEW

The *Titanic*'s band did not play for second- and third-class passengers, but this didn't stop steerage passengers from enjoying themselves. The *Titanic* provided a piano for them, and passengers brought aboard bagpipes and other instruments and played lively ragtime songs.

Charles Joughin: Chief Baker

Charles Joughin boarded the ship on April 4, 1912, well before its departure date. He was chief baker on board, with a staff of 13 working alongside him. He had served on the *Olympic* before joining the *Titanic* for her maiden voyage.

On the night of the sinking, Charles felt the collision and immediately got up to see what had happened. Once he realized crew members were readying the lifeboats, he sent each of his 13 men out with four 10-pound bread loaves to provision the boats. Food was not in short supply—the *Titanic* carried over 1,000 loaves of bread.

Joughin then proceeded to help load many of the boats. He refused a place in a lifeboat for himself when it was offered.

> **"THEY RAN AWAY FROM THE BOAT AND SAID THEY WERE SAFER WHERE THEY WERE."**
> (On placing reluctant women into lifeboats)

When he realized that all the boats were gone, Joughin headed toward B deck. There, he began throwing deck chairs into the ocean—his attempt to provide flotation devices to those in the water. With just minutes left before the ship completely flooded and sank, he climbed to the starboard side of the poop deck, threw himself over the railing, and rode the ship down "like an elevator." He recalled casually stepping into the water as the ship disappeared into the deep sea. His hair didn't even get wet. He was the last survivor to leave the *Titanic*.

While most people who plunged into the ocean panicked and thrashed about, Joughin calmly treaded water and swam for hours in the pitch black until the sun rose and he was able to spot an overturned lifeboat (collapsible B) in the distance. He swam toward it, but the survivors on it denied him help. There was no more room for another person. If they'd allowed him on the boat, it might've capsized.

Desperate for relief, Joughin floated to the other side of the boat, where fellow cook Isaac Maynard pulled him up just enough that only his feet and legs were left submerged.

When other lifeboats eventually came to the rescue, Joughin reported feeling colder in the open air on board than while he'd swum in the water. He was free of injury except for his feet, which were so swollen when he boarded the *Carpathia* that he was forced to climb the rungs of the rescue ladder with his knees.

While most froze to death within minutes, Joughin had managed to stay alive in the ice-cold water for hours. Although there are some theories about how he survived, nobody can truly explain how he lived through the bitter cold when so many others died so quickly.

WHO'S WHO

Isaac Maynard later claimed to have seen Captain Smith in his final moments. Smith was washed from the bridge and swam for safety. Another man on the overturned boat tried to reach out to the captain, but he refused the help, calling out, "Look after yourselves, boys."

WHO KNEW

During his final moments aboard, Joughin heard a mighty crash. He likely heard the ship breaking in half. The discovery of the separated ship in 1985 confirmed this theory.

Illustration of the separated front half of the *Titanic* on the seafloor

Lawrence Beesley:
Science Teacher

Beesley behind another passenger exercising in the gymnasium on the *Titanic*

N early everything known about the *Titanic* disaster came from those who managed to escape. One of the most thorough accounts came from Lawrence Beesley, a science teacher from the United Kingdom who boarded the *Titanic* as a second-class passenger. He was headed to America for vacation and was excited to travel on the largest ship ever built.

Just two months after the disaster, Beesley published a comprehensive account of his time aboard the *Titanic*, including the sinking. His observations were detailed. He painted a picture of lazy days enjoying meals, reading and writing in the library, and taking in sunrises and sunsets from high up on the decks. He explained how calm the waters were, how cold and brisk the air was.

Reading and writing room on the *Titanic*

Beesley was reading in his cabin on D deck when the collision occurred on the night of April 14. After four days at sea, he had gotten used to the movement of the ship, so although he didn't feel the crash, the sudden stillness warned him that something was wrong. As he explored the deck to find out why the engines had stopped, there was no sense of panic or urgency. Beesley went back to his room to dress—just in case—and continued to read.

Once it became clear there was an emergency, Beesley put on his lifebelt and headed toward the deck. He watched as people refused seats in lifeboats and others went back to their cabins, certain they were safer on the great ship than in a small boat.

Beesley was on the deck just above lifeboat 13 as it was lowered into the water with seats still empty. Crew members searched for women and children to fill the boats but couldn't find any. The officers in charge noticed Beesley looking over the railing and encouraged him to jump into the boat.

Beesley helped row the lifeboat a mile or two away from the ship and then watched as she went down. As the group in Beesley's lifeboat heard the shouts and watched hundreds of their fellow passengers struggling to stay afloat, they were stunned. Nobody on the lifeboat could believe what was happening, and they sat for hours in shocked silence while they waited for rescue.

Once aboard the *Carpathia*, passengers were frantic to inform loved ones of their survival. They wrote hundreds of wireless messages, but many were never delivered. Beesley's note detailing his survival was one of those undelivered telegrams. Nearly a week after the disaster, his name showed up on official missing persons lists, and friends published his obituary. It wasn't until his friends and relatives saw his firsthand reports in newspapers that they knew he had indeed made it out alive.

WHO KNEW

The boat deck, the highest of all, held the lifeboats, which had to travel almost 70 feet to the ocean below. After Beesley's lifeboat reached the water, the men in charge had a difficult time releasing the ropes from the ship. It took so long for them to move away from the ship that boat 15, which was being lowered above them, nearly crushed Beesley's lifeboat and all its occupants.

"THINK OF THE SHAME OF IT, THAT A MASS OF ICE OF NO USE TO ANYONE OR ANYTHING SHOULD HAVE THE POWER FATALLY TO INJURE THE BEAUTIFUL *TITANIC*!"

Eva Hart and Family: Second-Class Passengers

"Hold Mummy's hand and be a good girl." Those were the last words Eva Hart heard her father say. In 1912, seven-year-old Eva's family decided to emigrate from London, England, to Winnipeg, Manitoba, in Canada. The family initially planned to leave England by way of a different boat, but a coal strike in Southampton disrupted sailing schedules. Eva's family was offered passage to New York via the *Titanic*'s second class instead. Her mother felt uneasy about this change, and she said claiming a ship was unsinkable was "flying in the face of God." Nevertheless, the family agreed to change their plans.

When they boarded, Eva stood in awe of the *Titanic* towering above her. The young girl had never seen a boat before, and she could feel the excitement of everyone around her. One person who wasn't excited was her mother, who declared she knew something wasn't right. Because of her premonition, Mrs. Hart refused to sleep at night. Instead, she slept during the day and stayed awake while others slept. This decision may have saved her life.

During the first several days of the passage, Mrs. Hart stayed in her cabin, too seasick to eat or drink. Finally, on the morning of the sinking, Mrs. Hart felt well enough to venture out of her cabin and attend a Sunday church service with her family. They sang hymns and rejoiced about the safe passage so far.

That night, Mrs. Hart put little Eva to sleep and kept watch over the family. When the collision occurred, Mrs. Hart felt a small bump. Panicked, she woke her husband and insisted he investigate what had happened. Mr. Hart went to the decks to find out.

After he realized the situation, he rushed back to their room, wrapped Eva in a blanket, gathered his wife, and put on his warmest sheepskin coat. The family went straight to a lifeboat, where Eva and her mother were allowed to board. Mr. Hart threw the sheepskin coat over his wife's shoulders and uttered his final words to his daughter.

Eva and her mother watched in horror as the ship slowly slid into the Atlantic with her father still on board. Nightmares of the sight would haunt young Eva for years to come.

"THE WORST THING I CAN REMEMBER ARE THE SCREAMS. IT SEEMED AS IF ONCE EVERYBODY HAD GONE, DROWNED, FINISHED, THE WHOLE WORLD WAS STANDING STILL. THERE WAS NOTHING. JUST THIS DEATHLY, TERRIBLE SILENCE IN THE DARK NIGHT WITH THE STARS OVERHEAD."

Unlike many survivors, Eva was certain she had seen the *Titanic* split in half, an idea that many disputed up until the wreck's discovery in 1985. Once it was found, Eva was adamant that the site not be disturbed. Her father died on that ship, and she considered it his and the other victims' grave site.

Eva was a well-known *Titanic* survivor. She penned her autobiography in 1994 and granted many interviews to the press before she passed away in 1996.

WHO KNEW

A letter written by Eva and her mother was put up for auction in 2014, fetching $200,000. Mrs. Hart had written the note to her mother, with a short addition by Eva at the bottom, just after the church service on that last day at sea. When Mrs. Hart reached into her husband's coat pocket on the *Carpathia*, she discovered it there. The antique letter is the only surviving note written on *Titanic* letterhead while on board the doomed ship.

On board R·M·S·"TITANIC."

Sunday afternoon

My dear ones all,

As you see it is Sunday afternoon & we are resting in the Library after Luncheon. I was very bad all day Yesterday Could not eat or drink, & sick all the while, but today I have

...ince so far... long day & my week I ever... I must close... fondest love...

From your loving one

heaps of love and kisses to all from Eva x x x x x x x x x x x x x x x x x

Daniel Buckley: Third–Class Passenger

Being a male in third class on the *Titanic* meant near-certain death. Only 24 percent of third-class passengers survived, compared to 61 percent of first-class passengers. And only 20 percent of the ship's male passengers survived the sinking.

As one of the few third-class males to live, Daniel Buckley had a unique story, which he shared in detail during the US inquiry. While on board the *Carpathia*, the 21-year-old also penned a letter to his mother about the sinking. Both accounts became important testimony regarding the treatment of third-class passengers that night.

Buckley and six companions boarded the *Titanic* in Queenstown, Ireland. They were heading to New York from Ireland to fulfill a dream of starting a better life.

Buckley was asleep in his third-class berth when he was awakened by what he described as a "terrible noise." He jumped up, quickly realizing that water was seeping under the door. Buckley woke his three bunkmates, who thought he was joking. After all, they'd been told the *Titanic* was unsinkable.

> "I TOLD THE OTHER FELLOWS TO GET UP, THAT THERE WAS SOMETHING WRONG AND THAT THE WATER WAS COMING IN. THEY ONLY LAUGHED AT ME. ONE OF THEM SAYS: 'GET BACK INTO BED. YOU ARE NOT IN IRELAND NOW.'"

Eventually, Buckley convinced them to get dressed. Third-class quarters were cramped, so the young man stepped outside the room while his friends got ready. A steward passed by, shouting, "All up on deck! Unless you want to get drowned." Terrified, Buckley raced to the deck, forgetting his lifebelt back in his room. The *Titanic* was equipped with over 3,500 cork-filled lifebelts, more than enough for every passenger on board.

When he arrived on deck, Buckley spotted dozens of passengers wearing lifebelts. Realizing his mistake, he sped back down to his room. On his way, he encountered hordes of steerage passengers making their way up. When he finally arrived in steerage, Buckley came face-to-face with the water rushing into the ship, making it impossible for him to go down any farther.

Buckley returned to the deck desperately hunting for a lifebelt. Little did he know, the lifebelts would do scarcely more than keep passengers upright in the Atlantic as they froze to death. During his search, Buckley spotted a first-class passenger carrying two lifebelts. The stranger gave one to Buckley and helped him tie it around his body.

As the chaos on the decks grew, so did Buckley's fear. He watched as five lifeboats were lowered away, and he helped steady the ropes. Crew loaded lifeboat 13, and no more women and children stood nearby to fill the empty seats. A large crowd of men standing near Buckley jumped into the boat. Buckley dove in with them.

Just then, two officers came by with a cluster of steerage passengers. The officers ordered the men out of the boats so the women from the group could get on. Most of the men refused, so the officers drew their guns and shot into the air. That was enough of a warning to convince most of the men to leave.

As the shots rang out, Buckley began to cry, frozen with fear. A woman sitting next to him threw her shawl over his head, disguising him as a woman. The officers never spotted him. The group rowed away from the *Titanic* until the ship sank. When they finally spotted the *Carpathia*, the passengers lit letters on fire to create torches, waving them for the *Carpathia*'s crew to see. The survivors' cries of relief floated audibly over the water.

Lifebelts worn by *Titanic* survivors, on board the *Carpathia*

Buckley was one of only six men on board the lifeboat when it reached the *Carpathia*. But he was killed just six years after his lucky escape from the *Titanic*, while heroically serving in the US Army during World War I.

WHO KNEW

Debate remains about whether steerage passengers had equal access to lifeboats. According to Buckley, as he was heading up to the decks the first time, he encountered a sailor who told steerage passengers they weren't allowed up to first class. Another steerage passenger fought the man, pushing his way past. After this, Buckley never encountered anyone else preventing third-class passengers from accessing lifeboats.

Frank John Goldsmith: Third-Class Passenger

The Goldsmith family in 1906—Frank Jr. at left

There was no high tea, library time, or formal dinner for third-class passengers while on board the *Titanic*. Instead, third-class children like Frank Goldsmith were free to run about the ship and explore.

Frank John Goldsmith Jr. was only nine years old when the promise of a new, better life in America led the Goldsmith family to board the *Titanic*. Frank soon made friends with several other boys in third class. The group explored boiler rooms, watched firemen sing while they worked, and climbed baggage cranes.

Frank and his mother were asleep when his father felt the tremor of the ice fatally damaging the ship.

The sudden silence that overtook the halted ship alarmed him. When Frankie, his father, and his mother made their way upstairs, a steward stopped them and said only women and children could proceed to the boat deck. The men were forced to stay in third class, and Frank and his mother were separated from his father.

Frank didn't know it then, but as he proceeded to the deck, his father spoke his final words to him:

"MY DAD REACHED DOWN AND PATTED ME ON THE SHOULDER AND SAID, 'SO LONG, FRANKIE, I'LL SEE YOU LATER.' HE DIDN'T, AND HE MAY HAVE KNOWN HE WOULDN'T."

Frank and his mother finally reached a collapsible lifeboat, where they were some of the last passengers ushered to safety. Frank and his mother watched as the ship sank into the sea. Toward the end, his mother pressed his head into her body to prevent him from seeing the terrible scene unfolding. She didn't know that Frank was peering out from beneath her arm, watching the whole time.

One of the *Titanic*'s surviving firemen, Samuel Collins, befriended young Frank while they were on board the *Carpathia*. He showed him around the boilers of the ship and made him an honorary seaman—a member of the ship's crew. Samuel tried to soothe Frank's fears about his missing father by telling him, "Don't cry, Frankie. Your dad will probably be in New York before you are." Some people, like Collins, falsely believed that other ships also picked up survivors. Even after watching the *Titanic* disappear and finding out there were no other rescue ships, it took months for Frank to accept his father's fate.

Collapsible lifeboat carrying *Titanic* survivors

The memory of the disaster haunted Frank for the rest of his life. In adulthood, his family moved to a home near a baseball field, but the cheers of the crowd reminded him terribly of the cries of the *Titanic*'s dying passengers. He could never take his own children to a baseball game.

Frank left behind a legacy as a third-class *Titanic* survivor. He became an active member of the *Titanic* Historical Society, granted multiple interviews about his time on the *Titanic*, and shared his story in the only third-class survivor's memoir. When he died in 1982, his family spread his ashes over the last known location of the *Titanic*. He had always hoped to rejoin his father on its decks.

WHO'S WHO

Alfred Rush was a family friend who had joined the Goldsmiths on their voyage. The teenager turned 17 years old on April 14, 1912. When Alfred was offered a spot on a lifeboat, he refused, saying he wanted to stay back with the rest of the men. Recovery ships never found Alfred's body.

WHO KNEW

There were four collapsible lifeboats on board: two on the starboard side of the ship and two on the port side. Unlike the 16 wooden lifeboats, these vessels had heavy canvas sides that were quickly raised to form a boat. Each could carry 47 people.

Millvina Dean: Youngest Passenger

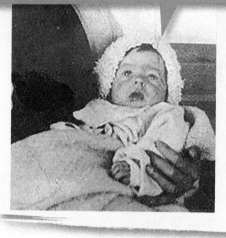

Millvina Dean had no personal recollection of being saved from a sinking ship. However, her experience on the *Titanic* cemented her place in history and altered the course of her long life. At just nine weeks old, Millvina was the youngest *Titanic* passenger. When she died in 2009, she was the ship's last living survivor.

The Dean family wasn't supposed to be on the *Titanic*. They had planned to travel on a different ship, but the coal strike changed that. Along with her mother and father, Millvina and her brother, Bertram, boarded the *Titanic* in Southampton as third-class passengers. The family was emigrating to Kansas.

Their dream of a new life in America would never become a reality.

On the night of April 14, 1912, Millvina's father shepherded her, her brother, and her mother to one of the first lifeboats full of third-class passengers. Mr. Dean never made it off the ship, and his body was never found.

Mourning her husband's death and without their family's breadwinner, Millvina's mother decided they would go straight back to England. Like many other survivors, they boarded a White Star Line ship, the *Adriatic*, where baby Millvina was a sign of hope—a miracle in the face of tragedy. Travelers waited in lines to hold her, deeming her "the pet of the voyage."

Millvina was eight years old when her mother told her she had been on the *Titanic* and revealed her father's fate. The disaster changed not only Millvina's family but also how her life unfolded. She grew up in Europe instead of Kansas.

"IF IT HADN'T BEEN FOR THE SHIP GOING DOWN. I'D BE AN AMERICAN."

As a young adult, Millvina spent most of her time out of the limelight. Millvina was in her seventies when Robert Ballard discovered the *Titanic* on the ocean floor, and she was one of only a handful of survivors left at that time. She participated in many *Titanic*-related events, appeared in multiple documentaries, and attended several *Titanic* Historical Society annual conferences.

The 1997 James Cameron film *Titanic* renewed interest in the ship. Millvina was again catapulted into the spotlight, but she never watched the movie. After viewing the first *Titanic* film, *A Night to Remember*, in 1958, she was plagued by nightmares, as she felt she could see her father on the screen in all the men scrambling on board the decks.

In her older years, Millvina turned to selling some of her most prized *Titanic* possessions in an attempt to raise money to pay her medical bills. She sold a suitcase that some kind New Yorkers had given her mother when they'd docked in the city after the sinking. The sale fetched more than $40,000.

Millvina passed away in 2009 at the age of 97. Her ashes were scattered in Southampton, at the port where she and her family had embarked on the maiden voyage that was never to dock.

WHO'S WHO

At 10 months old, Barbara Joyce West was the second-youngest passenger and the second-to-last living survivor. She, her mother, and her brother survived the sinking, but her father did not. Barbara resisted all media attention and never discussed it publicly. She often said she wanted nothing to do with "the *Titanic* people."

WHO KNEW

Many survivors boarded the White Star Line's RMS *Adriatic* on May 2, 1912, to return to England following the disaster. The *Adriatic* was a marvel at the time, boasting one of the first indoor swimming pools and **Turkish baths** aboard an ocean liner.

The swimming pool on board the *Titanic*

Jack Thayer:
First-Class Passenger

When all the survivors boarded the *Carpathia*, hundreds of women searched the decks for their lost friends and relatives. The search was often in vain, as many companions were forever lost at sea. Marian Thayer, however, reunited with her son, Jack.

Jack Thayer was only 17 when he boarded the *Titanic* at the port in Cherbourg. His first-class room was next door to his parents on C deck. When he noticed the sound of the *Titanic* colliding with the iceberg, he ventured up to the deck and told his mother that he was "going out to see the fun." Jack reported seeing a mass of ice in the distance and chunks of ice scattered on the deck. He saw that the *Titanic* was already beginning to list to one side, so he gathered his parents before heading to the boat deck. In the commotion there, he and his parents became separated. After a brief, unsuccessful search, he assumed they must have departed the ship via lifeboat.

Earlier that evening, Jack had met Milton Clyde Long, a fellow first-class passenger. After becoming separated from his family in the chaos, Jack stumbled upon his new friend. They were denied access to the lifeboats, and the boys watched as other passengers began jumping off the ship. The pair agreed it was their best bet. While Jack jumped away from the ship, Milton decided to slide down the side of the ship.

When Jack hit the bitterly cold water, he looked up to see one of the ship's large funnels teetering above him. It split away from the *Titanic* and crashed down into the ocean, missing Jack by only 20 feet. The suction of the sinking funnel pulled Jack deeper into the water. As he struggled to the surface, the debris field of the sunken ship surrounded him. He spotted an overturned lifeboat, collapsible B, and a stoker helped him onto it. Jack and the other men on the boat came face-to-face with three enormous propellers that rose high above the water. They were terrified that the blades would crush them, but soon the ship—and the propellers—did nothing more than slide quietly into the sea.

Jack was one of the very few males who survived after leaping off the ship and into the cold water. He never saw Milton again, but CS *Mackay-Bennett* found Milton's body.

Jack clung to the overturned lifeboat for hours, losing his grip and sliding into the sea several times. The men were finally rescued by lifeboats 4 and 12, the only two boats to return to pick up survivors. Officer Lightoller, also on the overturned boat, alerted the lifeboats with his whistle.

When Jack finally boarded the *Carpathia* around 8:30 the next morning, he was reunited with his mother, who frantically asked where his father was. Jack could only respond that he didn't know. Searchers never located his father's body.

On board the *Carpathia*, Jack and another passenger worked together to draw the now-famous images of the way the ship had split before it sank. Jack went on to publish several firsthand accounts of the sinking, including a 30-page pamphlet that he printed 500 copies of for his friends and family. The horror of the night never left him.

Drawing of the sinking of the *Titanic* made by Jack Thayer aboard the *Carpathia*

"THE SPECTACLE OF NEARLY 1,500 PEOPLE STRUGGLING IN THE ICE-COLD WATERS OF THE ATLANTIC, AND THE STEADY ROAR OF THEIR VOICES . . . IS A MEMORY THAT DOES NOT BECOME DIM, EVEN AFTER 20 YEARS."

WHO'S WHO

Charles Lightoller, also on lifeboat B, was the most senior officer to survive the sinking. He helped lower lifeboats until the last minute and was the last *Titanic* survivor to board the *Carpathia,* after making sure everyone else had reached safety.

WHO KNEW

The water temperature of the Atlantic on the night the *Titanic* sank is estimated to have been around 28 degrees Fahrenheit. Most passengers succumbed to hypothermia within 20 minutes. Lightoller described it as being "like a thousand knives being driven into one's body." Over 340 people who froze to death were recovered from the wreckage, still afloat with their lifebelts on.

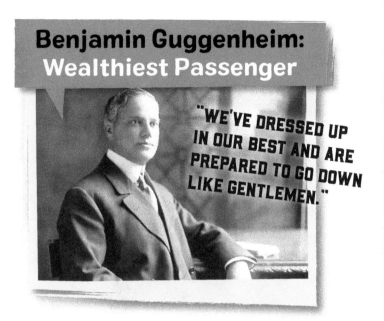

Benjamin Guggenheim: Wealthiest Passenger

"WE'VE DRESSED UP IN OUR BEST AND ARE PREPARED TO GO DOWN LIKE GENTLEMEN."

An American millionaire, Benjamin Guggenheim spent much of his time in France for business. He boarded the *Titanic* in Cherbourg and became one of the most well-known American victims of the disaster.

When the *Titanic* struck the iceberg, he was asleep in the same cabin as his valet, Victor Giglio. The men didn't awaken when the impact occurred; Guggenheim's traveling companions woke him 20 minutes after the fact.

Initially, Guggenheim put on his lifebelt and went to the deck to help load women and children onto lifeboats. His steward threw a sweater over him and encouraged him to stay on the boat deck and wait for a spot. Guggenheim saw his traveling companions off and said, "We will soon see each other again. It's just a repair. Tomorrow the *Titanic* will go on again."

However, Guggenheim quickly realized how severe the situation was and returned to his room with Giglio. The men put on their most elegant clothes and took off their

Replica of the Grand Staircase onboard the *Titanic*

lifebelts. They were last seen in the area of the Grand Staircase. Guggenheim stated, "We've dressed up in our best and are prepared to go down like gentlemen."

Days after the sinking, Guggenheim's grief-stricken wife heard a knock on her door. It was Mr. Guggenheim's bedroom steward, Mr. Henry Etches, who had survived as a crew member of lifeboat 5. Shortly before the sinking, the steward had encountered Mr. Guggenheim, who asked Etches to relay a message: "If anything should happen to me, tell my wife in New York that I've done my best in doing my duty."

WHO'S WHO

Helen Loraine Allison was the only first- or second-class child to die in the sinking. She'd boarded a lifeboat with her mother, Bess, but when Bess realized that her baby, Trevor, was missing, the pair ran all over the sinking ship, trying to find him. They didn't know that Trevor's nurse had already left with him in a lifeboat. Helen, Bess, and Helen's father were all lost in the sinking. Trevor was the only survivor in the family.

WHO KNEW

The *Titanic* and her sister ships required more than three million iron and steel rivets to hold the hull, **stern**, and **bow** together. After scientists recovered rivets from the wreckage, they conducted investigations into the metal's strength. The studies revealed that the material used in the rivets was subpar and brittle when exposed to freezing water. These weak rivets likely popped off when they made contact with the iceberg.

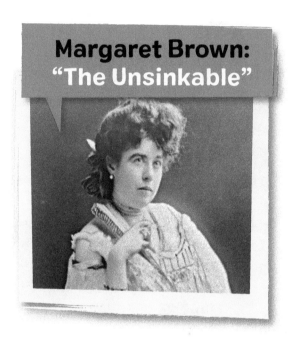

Margaret Brown: "The Unsinkable"

One of the most outspoken, well-known survivors was Margaret Brown, commonly known as the Unsinkable Molly Brown. Her parents were Irish immigrants to America. Margaret and her husband only escaped poverty after their marriage, gaining great mining wealth in the Colorado Gold Rush. Her humble upbringing and later success encouraged Brown to become involved in advocating for human rights. She stated, "Money can't make a man or woman.... It isn't who you are, nor what you have, but what you are that counts."

Brown boarded the *Titanic* in Cherbourg, rushing back from Europe to attend to a sick grandchild. After feeling the collision, she dressed in her warmest furs and made her way up to the deck to find lifeboats loading. Brown made sure other women and children were making their way to safety, and she resisted getting on a lifeboat before others. But while lowering the first lifeboat, a crew member picked up Brown and dropped her nearly four feet into it. Only 28 people found safety in lifeboat 6, which could have held 65.

After her lifeboat reached the sea, Brown realized there were only a few men on board, including Quartermaster Robert Hichens

Lifeboat carrying *Titanic* survivors

and Lookout Frederick Fleet. Margaret grabbed an oar and, with the help of other female passengers, rowed the boat as far out to sea as possible. Many feared the suction of a sinking ship would pull them down, so they rowed as far and fast as they could.

As panicked cries bellowed from the sinking ship, Margaret encouraged the lifeboat crew to turn back, as they had room to rescue more people. Hichens resisted this idea. He thought people trying to find safety on the boat would swamp them. Margaret pressed on, encouraging Hichens to turn back and attempt to pull survivors from the water. Despite her efforts, most historians don't believe lifeboat 6 went back to search for survivors.

"THE SPLASH OF THE OARS PARTLY DROWNED THE VOICES OF THE PERISHING ONES ON THE DOOMED STEAMER."

During the misery of the experience, Margaret held on to her mission to keep spirits up for everyone aboard lifeboat 6. Not only did she continue rowing, but she encouraged everyone to remain hopeful and work together.

On the *Carpathia*, Margaret Brown joined other first-class survivors to form the Survivors' Committee. She knew that many second- and third-class survivors had lost everything they owned. By the time the ship docked in New York, Brown's committee had already raised more than $10,000. Fluent in French, German, and Russian, Brown assisted survivors. She stayed on board the *Carpathia* until every survivor had been reunited with friends and family.

Brown quickly became the face of the survivors of the *Titanic*. Her factual eyewitness accounts helped piece together the terror that unfolded that night. Her selfless actions on the lifeboat and the *Carpathia*, and when she arrived in New York, earned her worldwide fame and branded her the heroine of the *Titanic*.

The official inquiries focused primarily on the men, and Margaret was appalled that they didn't interview her simply because she was a woman. She took matters into her own hands by writing her account of the sinking and giving lengthy newspaper interviews.

As the chairperson of the Survivors' Committee, she presented Captain Rostron and the entire crew of the *Carpathia* with medals of honor. For the rest of her life, Margaret continued to use her fame for good.

WHO'S WHO

Robert Hichens was the quartermaster at the ship's wheel when the *Titanic* struck the iceberg. He received the order to turn the ship "hard a'starboard" to attempt to steer away from the berg. Captain Smith then ordered Hichens to board the same lifeboat as Margaret Brown.

WHO KNEW

Only two lifeboats went back after the ship plunged into the ocean. Fifth Officer Harold Lowe transferred passengers from his boat to another to make space for survivors. Then he rowed back to the site in an attempt to rescue people from the water. However, the paralyzing temperature of the ocean had claimed most lives within minutes. Lowe's boat retrieved only four more survivors.

Noël Leslie, Countess of Rothes: First-Class Passenger

"THE INDESCRIBABLE LONELINESS. THE GHASTLINESS OF OUR FEELINGS NEVER CAN BE TOLD."

Noël Leslie, the Countess of Rothes, had devoted her life to charitable work but later became recognized for her role as another heroine of the *Titanic*.

The countess, along with her parents and her cousin Gladys Cherry, boarded the *Titanic* in Southampton. Leslie's parents left the ship when it stopped in Cherbourg, but she and her cousin continued onward toward America.

Leslie went to bed around 7:30 on the night of the sinking only to be startled awake by a jolt and the sudden eerie quiet of the ship. She looked at her watch, saw it was 11:46 p.m., and called to her cousin. When the pair went out to investigate, a steward told them the ship had grazed some ice and there was nothing to worry about.

As the cousins continued to explore, an officer rushed by. He demanded they put on their lifebelts and race to A deck. They headed back to their cabin. Dressed in their warmest clothes and with their lifebelts fastened, Leslie and Cherry rushed down the hall. Once they reached the deck, they boarded lifeboat 8.

The countess watched as Captain Smith ordered the seaman in charge of the lifeboat, Tom Jones, to "row straight for those ship's lights over there, leave your passengers on board, and return as soon as you can." Captain Smith was likely referring to the *Californian*, which was only 10 miles away. This order may have been his final effort to contact the ship, which wasn't responding to their distress calls.

As the cousins' lifeboat drifted away, the countess offered her assistance to the two crew members, making her way **aft** to steer the boat. Together, they rowed the boat as fast as they could, trying to reach the ship in the distance. When the countess suggested they turn back to try to rescue survivors, her idea was quickly shut down by most people in the lifeboat. The captain's order was to row for the distant ship.

When the *Titanic* finally lost its battle against the Atlantic, a young woman near Leslie screamed. Her husband was still on board. The countess did all she could to comfort the new widow.

The passengers and crew on lifeboat 8 rowed for three hours towards the lights of the other ship. All the while, Leslie and Jones encouraged the rest of the occupants and calmed their fears. When the *Carpathia* arrived, lifeboat 8 was the farthest away. Their commitment to rowing had taken them miles out to sea. Eventually they were rescued, and while on board the *Carpathia*, Leslie continued to help survivors by making clothes for babies and maintaining an encouraging spirit for all.

Upon her arrival in New York, the countess gave a detailed newspaper interview about her experience. People loved her story of female leadership, and she was hailed as a heroine by many on her lifeboat, including Tom Jones. Leslie claimed the two crewmen and the other passengers deserved just as much credit. She presented Jones and the other steward each with a silver pocketwatch as a show of gratitude, and Jones gave her the number plaque from their lifeboat. The two kept in touch until her death in 1956.

WHO'S WHO

María Josefa Peñasco y Castellana, a first-class passenger from Madrid, was the devastated widow the countess consoled in the lifeboat. María's mother-in-law had warned the newlywed couple against their trip on the *Titanic*, claiming a sea voyage was terrible luck for a honeymoon. To fool her into thinking they hadn't left Europe, their butler stayed in Paris, where he mailed prewritten postcards to trick her until they returned.

WHO KNEW

When the *Titanic* arrived in Cherbourg, her enormity required her to wait in deep water off the coast. The White Star Line's SS *Nomadic* was used to transfer first- and second-class passengers to the *Titanic* from the shore. The *Nomadic* is the only intact White Star Line vessel remaining. She is permanently docked in Belfast as a museum.

The SS *Nomadic*

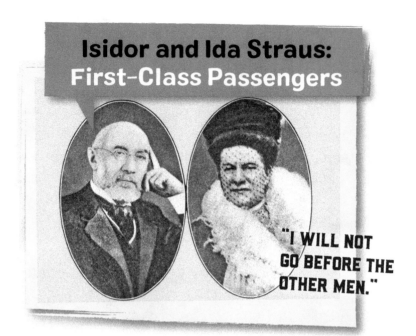

Isidor and Ida Straus:
First-Class Passengers

"I WILL NOT GO BEFORE THE OTHER MEN."

Isidor and Ida Straus were famous before the Titanic disaster, but after the sinking, everyone knew them for their story of bravery and love. Isidor was president of Macy's department store, and they were two of the wealthiest passengers on board the *Titanic*. Isidor had also served as a congressman representing New York State. Over their 41-year marriage, the Strauses raised seven children together in New York City. The two delighted in their family and traveling together and had an unbreakable love for each other.

As German immigrants, the couple always preferred to sail on German ships. However, in April

1912, Isidor and Ida Straus boarded the *Titanic* to return to America from a winter trip to France.

When the *Titanic* struck the iceberg, the couple fled to the lifeboats with their maid, Ellen Bird. Once they'd reached the deck, Ida and Ellen boarded a lifeboat. According to eyewitnesses, the officer in charge of loading the lifeboat said, "Well, Mr. Straus, you're an elderly man . . . and we all know who you are. . . . Of course you can enter the lifeboat with your wife."

Isidor couldn't stand the thought of leaving women and children behind. He rejected the offer, firmly stating that he would not leave the ship until all the women and children had spots on lifeboats. Nearby friends of the couple tried to convince Isidor that he should take the place on the lifeboat next to his wife and save himself. He refused.

Ida didn't hesitate. Upon hearing that her husband wouldn't join her, she leaped from the lifeboat back into his arms. "I will not be separated from my husband. As we have lived, so will we die—together," she cried. There was no use trying to convince Ida to leave the ship: She was determined to stay with her husband in death as she had in life.

Onlookers from the lifeboats watched the couple in their harrowing but peaceful final moments together. Ida and Isidor were last seen on the deck, tearfully embracing each other as the ship went down.

Fellow first-class passenger and friend Archibald Gracie, as well as Ida's maid, Ellen, shared their tale. Ellen recalled how thoughtful Ida was even in her last moments. Knowing it would be freezing in the lifeboats, Ida wrapped her young maid in her own fur coat and insisted that Ellen save herself.

Isidor's body was recovered and buried in the Straus Mausoleum in the Bronx, in New York City. Since Ida's body was never recovered, her family gathered water from the wreck site. They placed the water in an urn inside the mausoleum to honor the couple's dying wish—that they would never be apart.

The Straus Memorial

WHO KNEW

Shortly after the sinking, the White Star Line hired CS *Mackay-Bennett* to return to the scene of the wreck and recover the bodies left floating in the Atlantic. One hundred coffins, 100 tons of ice to store bodies, and **embalming supplies** for 70 bodies were on board the ship. The *Mackay-Bennett* recovered 306 of the 328 bodies that were found.

Sir Cosmo Duff-Gordon and Lady Duff-Gordon: First-Class Passengers

Lady Duff-Gordon

Lucy Christiana, Lady Duff-Gordon, and her husband, Sir Cosmo Edmund Duff-Gordon, were first-class passengers aboard the *Titanic*. In London Lady Duff-Gordon had built a fashion empire, while Sir Cosmo was an Olympic silver medalist. Unfortunately for the couple, their fame turned to infamy overnight.

The evening that the *Titanic* sank, Lady Duff-Gordon was offered a space in two lifeboats and turned down both, refusing to leave without her husband. She clung to him as they watched the decks clear. Suddenly, they noticed a smaller lifeboat that had plenty of space and nobody around to fill it.

Sir Cosmo knew this was their chance at survival. He asked the officer loading the boat if he, his wife, and their maid could board. The officer agreed, despite the rule about women and children only. The trio joined two other businessmen and seven seamen, and the crew lowered the boat. Only 12 people were on a lifeboat that was meant to save 40.

What happened next remains up for debate to this very day. According to the Duff-Gordons, they rowed far away from the *Titanic*. When they heard the shrieks of victims in the water, the group knew they were too far away to reach them in time.

As the hours passed, the couple took pity on the seven seamen who lamented their losses—not only their jobs but also many of their possessions. Sir Cosmo offered each of the men five **pounds** (about $760 today) to start anew. As soon as they got on the *Carpathia*, he wrote each of the men a check.

But according to newspaper reports, the couple had pushed their way into the boat, denying others a chance at survival. Sir Cosmo, a rich man, somehow secured a spot on a lifeboat amid hundreds of dying people, including women and children.

Their gesture of goodwill toward the seamen on the lifeboat wasn't out of kindness, the newspapers said—it was a bribe. The couple promised the men five pounds as a reward for not going back to rescue the screaming victims. They wrote the checks on the *Carpathia* and snapped a smiling picture surrounded by the men.

The press quickly got hold of the photo and reprimanded the couple for their merriment during such a monumental disaster. The Duff-Gordons returned to New York known as cowards, their lifeboat called the Money Boat.

The debate over what the couple actually did and what they should have done raged on for years. One fireman who was on their boat claimed the Duff-Gordons had pleaded not to return. Another crew member said no one ever discussed going back. Nobody could tell what was right.

"I HEARD NO SUGGESTION OF GOING BACK."
(Sir Duff-Gordon, on returning to rescue more passengers)

Due to the scandal and the small number of people who were saved on their boat, the Duff-Gordons were the only passengers interviewed for the British inquiry. It cleared the couple of all wrongdoing. The examination confirmed, though, that if the lifeboat had returned to the wreck, it likely would have saved many people.

Even with officials claiming the negative stories were false, the couple never escaped ridicule. Nearly every *Titanic* movie made has depicted the couple as greedy aristocrats.

Almost 100 years after the tragedy, surviving relatives of the Duff-Gordons discovered a box of documents labeled "*Titanic*." It contained letters the couple had written to family members and other narratives of the sinking. Their living relatives hope that with this new evidence, the couple's names will finally be cleared.

WHO'S WHO

An everlasting image ingrained in the minds of those who have studied the *Titanic* is one of a young boy holding an *Evening News* poster that reads, "Titanic Disaster Great Loss of Life."

The boy's name was Ned Parfett, and the photograph was taken just outside the White Star offices in London. Sadly, Parfett died in World War I only six years after the *Titanic* disaster.

WHO KNEW

The emergency lifeboat the Duff-Gordons boarded was one of two that were already swung out from the rail to make launching them quick and efficient. The ship had one of these boats on each side, and lifeboat 1 boarded from the starboard side. These smaller boats were called captain's boats, as they were often used to serve the crew in emergencies, such as a man going overboard.

Captain Arthur Rostron:
Captain of the *Carpathia*

On the night of the tragedy, the *Carpathia*, a Cunard Line ship, was cruising in the opposite direction of the *Titanic* with more than 700 passengers on board. At 12:15 a.m., its commander, Captain Rostron, was asleep when his wireless operator on duty, Harold Cottam, rushed into his cabin to report the *Titanic*'s distress message. Rostron flew into action.

Reaching the *Titanic*'s last known location was filled with the same dangers that had caused the collision in the first place. Icebergs and small ice growlers surrounded the ship. Captain Rostron posted extra lookouts to spot dangers and to assist in maneuvering the ship around the ice. The *Carpathia* was 58 miles away from the scene of the disaster and cruising at around 14 knots per hour. Rostron increased the speed to the maximum of 17.5 knots. The crew turned off the heat and hot water so all the steam could drive the engines at full speed. Every stoker was awakened to shovel coal and fuel the furnaces.

"I CAN ONLY CONCLUDE ANOTHER HAND THAN MINE WAS ON THE HELM."
(On how he sped quickly and safely through dangerous conditions)

Even with these orders in place, it took the ship three and a half hours to reach the *Titanic*'s last known location.

In anticipation of their arrival at a sinking ship, Rostron ordered his staff to prepare their lifeboats. Officers lowered ladders and riggings to help pull people from the water. Cargo cranes were readied to lift luggage and lifeboats from the sea. Stewards organized blankets, food, and drinks. The ship's three doctors turned the dining rooms into medical wards. Crew were stationed in hallways to calm the *Carpathia*'s worried passengers. When all preparations were complete, Rostron encouraged his crew to stop for coffee. He knew the day would be long.

Despite their preparations, nobody on board the *Carpathia* knew what to expect when they arrived at the scene. Communication with the *Titanic* had ended abruptly hours before, so they had prepared for every possibility. But they never imagined the tragedy that awaited.

As Rostron's ship got closer to the *Titanic*'s position, he ordered green rockets to be shot into the air. He hoped this would alert the occupants of the sinking ship that they were getting closer. Those rockets instead let the 700 passengers in lifeboats know that help was nearby.

They loaded the first survivors onto the ship at 4:10 a.m. Rostron asked crew members where the *Titanic* was. Gone, they said. She was gone.

With all known survivors on board, Rostron had to decide where to go. He wanted to continue onward to Europe, but he didn't have enough supplies for all on board. Halifax, Canada, was the closest destination, but that would require traversing ice fields. With all of this in mind, and after consulting with White Star's managing director, Bruce Ismay, the *Carpathia* set course back to New York.

As they neared New York City, tugboats carrying reporters pulled up alongside the ship, shouting questions to the survivors through megaphones. Family members scrambled for news of loved ones. The *Carpathia* had never received so much attention.

Titanic survivors on board *Carpathia* after their rescue

The *Titanic*'s survivors praised Captain Rostron and his crew for their valiant efforts. Shortly after they arrived in New York, the Survivors' Committee presented *Carpathia* crew members with medals and

Captain Rostron with a gold cup. Rostron continued to work at sea for many years, staying out of the spotlight and never taking credit for his role on that early morning.

WHO KNEW

Around 8:00 a.m. on April 15, the *Carpathia* met the *Californian*, which was 5 to 10 miles away from the *Titanic*. When the *Titanic* sank, the *Californian* had stopped for the night due to the dangers of ice, and her wireless operator had gone to bed. It wasn't until 5:00 the following morning that the *Californian* learned of the tragedy—and thus the many lives she could have saved—via wireless message. When the *Californian* finally arrived at the wreck site, Captain Rostron ordered her to stay nearby and look for survivors, but she found none.

GLOSSARY

aft: toward the back, or stern, of the ship

boat deck: where lifeboats are stored on a ship and where they are launched from

bow: the front end of a ship

bridge: the forward part of a boat deck, where the ship is commanded from; provides a clear view over the front end of the ship and is directly in front of the wheelhouse, where the main steering equipment is housed

CQD: a common distress call used on Marconi wireless radios that meant "all stations: distress"

crow's nest: a tall structure that extends above the ship and serves as the lookout's watch point

deck: The *Titanic* had 10 decks that functioned like different floors of the ship. The topmost, the boat deck, had areas for promenading, the bridge, and the lifeboats. Deck A, also known as the promenade deck, had special entertainment areas for first-class passengers. Decks B through F were passenger decks, and decks G and below contained essential machinery like the engine and boiler rooms.

embalming supplies: supplies used to preserve deceased bodies and prepare them for burial

forecastle deck: the forwardmost upper deck on the ship

forward: toward the front, or bow, of the ship

founder: when a ship fills with water and sinks

hull: the main body of a ship, including the bottom, sides, and decks

keel: the middle line that runs along the bottom of the boat

lifebelt: a personal flotation device designed to keep a person afloat in water, also called a life vest; the *Titanic*'s were made from cork

lifeboat: small boats that can be lowered into the ocean in case of an emergency

liner: a ship that carries passengers across the ocean, typically along a regular route; also known as a "passenger liner" or "ocean liner"

officer: a person in charge of manning the ship and always present on the bridge

port: a harbor where ships dock; also refers to the left side of a ship

pound: currency used in the United Kingdom at the time of the sinking

sister ships: ships of the same class with nearly identical design; the three luxury liners the *Olympic*, the *Titanic*, and the *Britannic* were sister ships

starboard: the right side of a ship

steerage: a term that was interchangeable with "third class" and whose tickets were the least expensive

stern: the rear of a ship

steward: a crew member in charge of taking care of the passengers on board a ship

stoker: a fireman who kept the boilers powered

Turkish bath: a spa facility with steam rooms, massage suites, cool rooms, and more; on the *Titanic*, it was exclusively for the use of first-class passengers

RESOURCES

SOCIETIES AND MUSEUMS

Titanic Historical Society, Indian Orchard,
    Massachusetts

Titanic International Society, New Jersey

Titanic Museum, Branson, Missouri

Titanic Museum, Pigeon Forge, Tennessee

Titanic Belfast, United Kingdom

SS *Nomadic*, Belfast, United Kingdom

Premier Exhibitions, *Titanic*: The Artifact Exhibition

Titanic cemeteries, Halifax, Nova Scotia

WEBSITES

Encyclopedia Titanica (Encyclopedia-Titanica.org)

Titanic Inquiries (TitanicInquiry.org)

Titanic Facts (TitanicFacts.net)

Titanic (Titanic-Titanic.com)

BOOKS

A Night to Remember by Walter Lord

The Story of the Titanic *as Told by Its Survivors* by
    Lawrence Beesley, Archibald Gracie, Commander
    Lightoller, and Harold Bride

The Loss of the SS Titanic: *Its Story and Its Lessons* by
  Lawrence Beesley
Titanic *Survivor* by Violet Jessop
Titanic *Eyewitness: My Story* by Frank J. W. Goldsmith
The Discovery of the Titanic by Dr. Robert D. Ballard
Sinking of the Titanic: *Eyewitness Accounts* edited by
  Jay Henry Mowbray
Titanic by Leo Marriott
Titanic: *An Illustrated History* by Don Lynch

MEDIA

National Geographic: Secrets of the Titanic: *A Legend
  Surrenders Her Mysteries*
Titanic: *The Complete Story* (The History Channel)
A Night to Remember

ACKNOWLEDGMENTS

Thank you to my husband and girls, who listened to my endless *Titanic* tales and supported the hours of research and writing. David, thank you for all the *Titanic* teas, dinners at the Molly Brown House, and enduring the nonstop *Titanic* viewings. To my parents, for never batting an eye at my sometimes over-the-top obsession. To my students who stood in awe as I enthusiastically told the story of the *Titanic*. To all the teachers, parents, and historians who continue to teach the story to children and help ensure that the *Titanic*'s memory lives on. Many thanks to Marty Talbert, a fellow *Titanic* buff to whom I reached out as a young girl. I'll be forever appreciative of the survivor autographs, photographs, paper clippings, and inspiration.

ABOUT THE AUTHOR

 **MARY MONTERO** is a teacher, avid *Titanic* enthusiast, and the teacherpreneur behind Teaching with a Mountain View. After becoming captivated by the story of the *Titanic* at the age of eight, she made it her mission to pass on the tale to her own students. She created an experience-based class centered solely around the *Titanic*, attends an annual *Titanic* dinner at the Molly Brown House, and is a member of the *Titanic* Historical Society. She's always sure to tell people that her love for the great ship began long before the *Titanic* movie was released, even if it's rare for a day to pass that she doesn't quote the movie in casual conversation.